PRAISE FOR ANDREA GIBSON

"Andrea Gibson's work looks likes poetry, and sounds like poetry, but feels like something much larger, more expansive."

—Posture

"Gibson's poems are forthright and pithy, putting into words the feelings of anyone who has been angry, or outraged, or embarrassed, or in love."

—Star Tribune

"Andrea Gibson's work shows up to your door without any pretension. It gives, pushes, and asks, knowing that even its beauty cannot answer it all. Each poem is a small fire signaling home, and home happens to be ourselves. Gibson has generously given us a blissful surrender to the immensity known as love."

—Yesika Salgado, author of *Corazón*

"With such tenderness and empathy and humor, Andrea Gibson's *You Better Be Lightning* does such important dreaming work, visioning work, looking work, in this stunning collection of generous poems. Of these poems' infinite superpowers, my favorite might be their use of anecdotes as a sort of beckoning, welcoming a reader into this book's lush ecosystem of intimacy. Read these poems and feel held, welcomed, forgiven."

— Safia Elhillo, author of *The January Children*

YOU BETTER BE
LIGHTNING

YOU BETTER BE LIGHTNING

Andrea Gibson

BUTTON PUBLISHING INC.

MINNEAPOLIS

2021

Published by Button Poetry / Exploding Pinecone Press

Minneapolis, MN 55403 | http://www.buttonpoetry.com

Cover design: Amy Law

ISBN 978-1-943735-99-0

Ninth Printing

For Manny—
when I'm riding on the handlebars
out of the pitch dark, your light
is pedaling.

Contents

1   Acceptance Speech after Setting the World Record in Goosebumps

5   The Year of No Grudges, *or* Instead of Writing a Furious Text,
    I Try a Poem

10   The Museum of Broken Relationships

16   Time Piece

22   Queer Youth Are Five Times More Likely to Die by Suicide

26   No Such Thing as the Innocent Bystander

27   To Whom It Definitely Concerns,

29   Every Time I Ever Said I Want to Die

32   Instead of Depression

33   What Love Is

36   Homesick: a Plea for Our Planet

40   The Day Prince Died

43   My Gender Is the Undoing of Gender

45   Spelling Bee Without Stinger

46   The Night Shift

50   Love Me to Life

53   Love Letter to the Tick that Got Me Sick

57   After the Break-Up, Our Tandem Bike Speaks:

59   Neighbors

63   Note to the Stranger Six Feet Away:

64   Good Grief

65   The Call, Option 1

70   The Call, Option 2

73   What Can't Be Taken

74   The Test of Time

78   Aliens Explain Why They Are Visiting Earth

81   Constellations Rearrange Themselves into a Protest Sign

82   Climate Change

84   Wellness Check

85   My Girlfriend's Karaoke Song

88   What You Wish You'd Said to the High School Guidance Counselor

90   What Sucks About the Afterlife

92   How the Worst Day of My Life Became the Best

95   Life Sentence

96   Not Alone

99   How I Became a Poet

104   See This Through

108   The Last Hours

113   Acknowledgements

115   About the Author

YOU BETTER BE
LIGHTNING

ACCEPTANCE SPEECH AFTER SETTING THE WORLD RECORD IN GOOSEBUMPS

I wasn't, by any means, a natural.
Was not one of those wow-hounds
born jaw-dropped. I was tough in the husk.
Went years untouched by rain. Took shelter

seriously, even and often especially
in good weather, my tears like teenagers
hiding under the hoods of my eyes,
so committed they were to never falling

for the joke of astonishment.
When I was told there were seven
wonders of the world, I trusted the math,
believed I had seen none of them.

Of course beauty hunted me.
It hunts everyone. But I outran it, hid
in worry, regret, the promise of an afterlife
or a week's end.

Then one day, in a red velvet theater
in New Orleans, I watched Maya Angelou
walk on stage. Seventeen slow steps to the mic.
She took a breath before speaking,

and I could hear god being born in that breath.
My every pore reached out like a hand
pointing to the first unsinkable lotus in the bayou
of the universe. I'd never felt anything like it.

Searched the encyclopedia for the feeling's name
when I got home: "Goosebumps."
Afterward, I thought—*I can do this.*
Started training morning to night,

crowbar swinging like a pendulum at the wall
of my chest. Tore the caution tape off
my life and let everything touch it:

Allen Iverson on the television in his first season
with the Sixers, crossover sharp as a V of sparrows
flying through the paint like Michelangelo's brush:
        333 goosebumps.

My baby sister, sober for the first time
in thirteen years, calling to tell me she just noticed
our mother's eyes are green:
        505 goosebumps.

One day, my friend scored tickets
to a Prince concert. Tiny venue. I was right
behind the sound booth. Prince's entire band
that evening—women. At the end of the show,
the sound person turned around and whispered,
He didn't play one song on his setlist the whole night.
I live on stages. I know what it is to scratch a plan
but not the whole trip and still arrive to your destination
two hundred years before your time:
        421 (artists formerly known as) goosebumps.

But that's just the fancy stuff.
Some of them came from simple facts—
it rains diamonds on Jupiter:
        189 goosebumps.

Blood donors in Sweden receive
a thank-you message when their blood is used:
    301 Nordic goosebumps.

One night in Ann Arbor, my friend,
still undiagnosed, could not uncurl her fingers
to strum her guitar, so she sang the chords instead.
It was the first time in my life I'd seen pain
become an instrument:
    10 dozen goosebumps

for each and every note plucked
from the string section of her refusal to silence
her dream. After that, nothing in the world was gray.
Even the movie of my past was released in color.
The oldest man in my hometown could not
get to the door to listen to our carols,
so we went inside and sang at his bedside instead.
Twenty-four boots on the front step
catching snowflakes with their tongues:
    776 goosebumps.

At one point everything started doing it:
A sincere apology: 221 goosebumps.
An enemy's love poem: 222 goosebumps.

The moon rising over the continental divide.
My girlfriend and I thought it was a car
driving off a cliff, and suddenly nothing
in the world was dying. You ever felt that?
A split second when nothing in the world is dying?
    888 goosebumps,

and the next day I sharpened a tiny ax
so I could split the seconds myself.

Too much lives in a moment
to not feed it to the fire in the heart, slow.
A Missoula treehouse filled with candlelight:
   143 goosebumps.

The octopus documentary:
   54 goosebumps, multiplied by 8.

The biggest dog in the shelter
hiding behind a teacup chihuahua,
and the woman who came to adopt a cat
taking all three of them home:
   1,012 goosebumps.

There is no escaping the magic now.
Beauty caught me and never let me go.
And the thing about the world record
is—if someone breaks it after me,
and they *will* break it after me,
I will love that so much
that without even trying,

   I'll break it again.

THE YEAR OF NO GRUDGES, OR
INSTEAD OF WRITING A FURIOUS TEXT, I TRY A POEM

I know most people try hard
to do good and find out too late
they should have tried softer.

I've never in my whole life
been levelheaded, but the older I get,
I'm more level-hearted—

and I think we make gods
who look like us for a reason.
I think, in spite of it all, we trust

we can be believed in.
When I don't believe in myself,
I try to remember I have walked

on water, like, seven-hundred times
in Maine in the dead of winter.
Where I come from, you can drive

a pickup truck from one side
of the lake to the other, and people
have an unusually high quantity

of missing teeth and fingers,
but you can still count on them
to buy whitening strips and wedding rings

because where I come from
beauty is in the eye of anyone who sees
what's missing but can't stop pointing

to what's still there.
If there's no definition for love yet—
I think that's a good one.

I'm writing you, Friend, on a day
you did me wrong. I'm only half
a second outside the furnace of my rage,

and I'm trying to focus
my attention on all the teeth
you still have, the teeth

I know you'd happily knock out
yourself if it would keep you
from biting anyone again.

That's how mistakes work
if you're loving the right kind of people.
And you're the right kind of people.

You've walked on water
so many times you know grace
is super, super slippery.

There's literally nothing
anyone is more likely
to fall from.

Some sound advice I give myself,
like, twice an hour: *Wear knee pads*
on the way to your ego, Andrea.

Being right is boring.
It comforts only the tiniest
parts of us, and when it comes to hearts,

I want to always be a size queen
'cause that's how I found you—
lifting the spirits of everyone around

like a hot air balloon
just from the way you burned
to be a better person today

than you were the day before.
Burning to be better is my favorite
quality on anyone, and you are on fire

like a gay men's choir
rocking the halftime show
of a football game.

I've been dancing in the end zone
since you taught me to start breaking
every promise I have made

to my pain, taught me my wounds
will never be bigger than I am.
Thank goodness for you,

champion of the unkillable *YES*,
dandelion refusing to be cut
for the bouquet.

Five minutes into our first conversation
you knew I could take a punch
better than I could take a compliment

and you talked to me about it only once
and *BAM!* I was angel gossip.
There were god-rumors spreading

in my suddenly un-heavied head.
I love you because you've never had a mirror
face. Because the truth is the last thing

you would ever try to fake.
So sometimes you look like a human
scribble, like a two-year-old

has colored you in,
like you have too many feelings
to stay inside the lines

of your own skin. But that, my friend,
is the masterpiece. I love you
because we have both showed up

to kindness tryouts
with notes from the school nurse
that said we were too hurt to participate.

But we learned how wrong we were,
and weren't those the best days?
The days we learned how wrong we were

and so got to grow
into our goodness, throwing
the peach pits of our old selves

into the garden to grow sweetness.
Sugar, I pick you to be the captain
of my chosen family tree.

I pick you to throw the party
when I leave this world
knowing I'm gonna run death

like a stop sign
and keep going.
I pick you to finish

all my half-written poems
even though you suck
at writing poetry.

I pick you to finish this one
especially, which is basically
just a list of compliments

you'd be a hypocrite not to take,
so take it before I remember:
I'm mad at you, Asshole,

Butt Knuckle, Nutwad,
only human on Earth
who knows exactly what I mean

when I say *god*—I mean everyone
down here who understands why
when I get to heaven,

I will refuse to call it heaven
if the people I love
(who put me through hell)

aren't there.

THE MUSEUM OF BROKEN RELATIONSHIPS

In Croatia, in 2006, Olinka and Drazen broke up.
Having no idea what to do with the relics
from the four years of their love, they created
the Museum of Broken Relationships.

For years now they've been collecting items
from the broken-hearted all over the world.
Each day, treasures arrive at the museum's door:
a small bottle of a lover's tears.

The last checkbook with both partners' names.
A shiny watch with the pin pulled out
the second he said *I love you* for the first time.
In the Museum of Broken Relationships

there is a toaster. Beside it, a note:
When I moved across the country
I took the toaster. That will show you.
How are you going to toast anything now?

In another display there is a cell phone.
Written beside it, the words: *He gave me*
his own cell phone so I couldn't
call him anymore.

There is a letter *T* from a keyboard
from a couple whose online passion died
after their first real-life encounter.
The keyboard taken apart in a commitment

to never again trust a computer key
to open one's heart. In the Museum
of Broken Relationships, you can find a letter
from a thirteen-year-old boy to his first love in Sarajevo

written before leaving to escape the war.
You can find an air sickness bag
from a couple whose relationship did not survive
the turbulence of long distance.

You can find an ax used to chop the furniture
of a partner who had an affair, giving new
traumatic meaning to the phrase
splitting up.

There is a jar of Love Incense
with a note that says, *It simply
doesn't work.* There is a display case
with a pair of papier-mâché breasts

gifted by a woman whose husband
insisted she wear them during sex:
They were bigger than mine, she said.
They turned him on, and I left.

And in the Museum of Broken
Relationships in Croatia, there are three
juggling balls sewn by hand,

by my hands, from material
cut from my socks, you say,
though I am certain

it was my underwear.
Either way, the juggling balls
were made from what I wore

underneath what everyone could see
and sewn with precision
the way my grandma taught me

before dying of a broken heart
and leaving me a collection of thimbles
so I could be someone

strong enough to keep things
from falling apart.
The first time I saw you

I fell apart.
I had no idea who you were.
You walked into a studio I was in

and walked out.
Minutes later I was a puddle
in the parking lot,

my friend's hand on my back
asking what was wrong.
I couldn't explain it.

It was 2003.
I had no woo-woo in me
back then. I didn't believe

in reincarnation.
I just knew I'd loved you once
and would again. Months later,

still not knowing who you were,
I saw you on TV reporting the invasion
of Iraq, then the occupation of Palestine,

a bloodfire in the sky above you
and you not flinching,
or I thought you weren't flinching

until we started sharing a bed
and I could see the war
behind your eyelids,

how you tore the covers off
every morning like a kid
unwrapping a gift.

Like the dawn of a simple day
was everything you'd ever
put on your Christmas list.

I'd still be sleeping when you'd leave
for circus practice. Circus practice,
where you'd walk the tightrope, twirl

on trapeze bars, then come home
and pull me into the front yard to teach me
how to toss juggling balls

into a still-blushing sky.
When I think about why we broke up,
why you flew all the way to Croatia

to let go of the juggling balls I made you,
I know it's because I was a terrible juggler.
I couldn't figure out how to hold something

and set it free at the same time.
So I dropped the ball. Convinced myself
I was up in the air about you

when really I was up in the air about me.
It's what we do—turn our bodies into museums
of what was broken. Blame

the checkbook, the affair, the bottled up
tears. Blame the toast going stale
the day after the wedding.

We rip the letter off the keyboard
instead of *control, command, escape, delete.*
Say it was the turbulence

of long distance instead of the baggage
unclaimed. But at the carousel of clarity
(otherwise known as fifteen years of therapy),

I see I wasn't running from the war
back then. I was running from the peace.
The love I did not believe I was worth.

And because that lie held so much grief,
I don't know that I ever got over you
as much as I got under

the engine of myself
to fix the machine of my love,
which now runs okay

but still runs way too much,
if you know what I mean,
and I know you know what I mean,

because this was not the first lifetime
we said goodbye
without wanting to say goodbye,

was it?

TIME PIECE

I've never known who Nick is.
I show up just in the stranger of time,
sift every grain of sand from the Pacific Coast
into an hourglass that fits in my palm.

I turn the hourglass upside down and Vancouver
trades places with San Diego. When they ask how
I covered the wildfires in snow, I say
I had time on my hands.

      * * *

My grandfather was a clock
who stopped before I met him.
I've heard he was so kind
you could look into his face

and know you'd never been late
for anything. My mother is still
a little girl riding on his shoulders.
Time flies and she reaches up

to pluck feather pens
from its wings so I can write
this life down. I try.
But it doesn't stay down.

It keeps flying so fast I count
my wrinkles the way I used to
count sheep. When the number
gets high enough, I'm told I'll fall

asleep forever, but:

I once watched a woman skip
her gravestone across a lake
like a smooth pebble. Death hops
if you let go at the right time.

The Buddha says
the right time is always now.

                * * *

My father calls me on the phone
and before I can say hello, asks,

*Do you know what Steve Jobs said
the instant before he died?
He said, WOW!*

Time is money.
But the end of money
is *wow*.

                * * *

My friend wakes up at noon.
Goes to bed at eight. Wants less time
because she wants less pain.

I understand. I've been there too.
I can spot a scar beneath a wristwatch
from a hundred yards away.

And no, it is not the weak who try
to clock out early. It's people
who are desperate to go home.

                    * * *

Einstein says time is relative.
Says the higher you get above sea level,
the faster time goes. I live in Colorado.
My house is over a mile into the sky.
All day I hear the wheels of time
burning rubber on the clouds,
my life in a getaway car, racing
toward the border, which is an invisible line

I only call *death* when I forget how to speak
eternity's language, forget that to run
out of time is to run into the truth
that none of us have ever been
our bodies. If we were—how
would we fit in each other's hearts?

                    * * *

To make up for lost time,
you do not need to know why
time went missing, or what

kidnapped it, or if its face
was on back of a milk carton
every day for fifteen years.

To make up for lost time, you need
only to put down the grudge
you are holding so you can pick up

the phone and say, *How many days*
did we need each other at the same time
without knowing it?

Bitterness is the easiest way
to leave this world having had only
a near-life experience.

        * * *

My partner and I have had hard days.
Hard months. But time stops

when you're in love,
so I am the same age

as I was when we met
five years ago.

She makes time for me
with her own hands, builds me

a watch from the silver
that hasn't yet grown in my hair.

Beside her I've learned
that the only real way

to waste time, to drag
the seconds to the curb,

to fill the landfill
with minutes,

is to let my body

be a time capsule

I forget to put my heart in.

* * *

Don't forget to put your heart in.

Regret is a time machine to the past.
Worry is a time machine to the future.
Gratitude is a time machine to the present.

No one books my travel for me.
I decide where I want to go.

I decide if I will be a sculptor
carving out time the way that Michelangelo
carved the statue of David

after two other artists gave up
on that same block of marble, citing
its poor quality, its impossible brittleness.

All time is quality time.
Don't abandon your chisel
believing it's not.

* * *

No matter how it looks,
you and everyone you know
have hourglass figures.
Each breath, a falling
grain of sand.

To truly live is to see
right through the skin
to the avalanche.

If we never deny
the inevitable end
of the story,
we will write it
more beautiful
while we're alive.

QUEER YOUTH ARE FIVE TIMES MORE LIKELY TO DIE BY SUICIDE

means:
You lived five times harder than you should have had to
to still have a body when you graduated high school.

means:
Hate worked five times harder
to make your spirit its wishbone.

means:
When your mother asked what was wrong,
you were five times more likely to believe you'd lose
her if you spoke the truth.

means:
You were told five times more often
you'd go to hell when you died.

means:
Burning for eternity seemed five times
more doable than another day in the school lunchroom.

means:
You were five times more inclined
to triple-padlock your diary.

means:
You were five times more likely
to stop writing your story down.

means:
I write my heart out now.

I graffiti billboards with the page of my diary
the bullies used to start the rumors.

I tie that page to the end of a kite string and run
a crooked line through the straightest mile
of the Bible Belt.

That page is a protest sign.
That page is a bandana washing
the tear gas out of my lover's eyes.

Queer youth are five time more likely to die by suicide

means:
I sneak into fascist sleepovers
and sharpie my pronouns onto the faces
of senators who voted to criminalize my kisses
when I was nineteen.

I cut the hate out of my mail
and papier-mâché Christmas ornaments
for queer couples whose parents
do not want to know their grandchildren.

I hack high school curriculums and delete
every test that does not ask what the P
in Marsha P. Johnson stands for.

I walk through graveyards with a chisel
correcting the names of trans kids
whose families said, *No*, when asked,
Can you just let me live?

I pace the suburbs with spray paint, editing
the welcome mats of homophobes until they all

speak the truth: that they personally burned
the roof over the heads of *queer youth*
are five times more likely to die by suicide

means:
There are many days I thirst for my own silence
but walk through the desert screaming instead
because I, like most of my queer friends, don't have a child
—I have millions—from Nebraska to Chechnya,

to the Baptist church where I grew up.
My pride in them is a parade I know
won't keep all of them alive, but I keep cutting
my diary into confetti to throw at their hopes

when they float by scared or furious
or laughing or in love and desperate
for the headline to say: *Queer youth*
are five times more likely to:

offer to walk their younger siblings home from school.
To notice the different accents of sparrows.
To find an eyelash and spend twenty minutes
trying to pick what to wish for.

Five times more likely to:

never outgrow blanket forts.
To know there is a word for the scent in the air
after it rains. To see lifelines look like telephone wires
and call a friend who's having a bad day.

Five times more likely to:

adore the last man who walked on the moon
just because he wrote his daughter's initials there.
To know there is no universe in which they would not
be proud of their own children.

Queer youth are five times more likely to:

see you how you dream of seeing yourself.
To write something in your yearbook that will get you
through the next decade. To spot a stranger crying
and ask if there's anything they can do to help.

Five times more likely to:
need us to do the same.

NO SUCH THING AS THE INNOCENT BYSTANDER

Silence rides shotgun
wherever hate goes.

TO WHOM IT DEFINITELY CONCERNS,

please accept this letter as formal notification that I am resigning from the position of My Own Worst Enemy. I've appreciated the opportunity to lower my standards so far they could win a limbo contest against a crumb. I've been honored to serve as the server at the banquet where I eat myself alive. The day I was hired I could never have imagined how many employee-of-the-month plaques I'd acquire from breaking the standing record for standing in my own way.

In this position I've grown continuously, like bacteria in a staph infetion. I had no idea that holding myself back would be contagious. I would like to have a different kind of impact on the future company I keep. The scene I made during our last team building exercise woke me to the need for a change. I know the young people in the office are still shaken by my refusal to catch myself in the trust fall. I apologize for that gory display.

Moving forward, I'll be pursuing opportunities in another field, preferably one where break rooms are for resting and not for breaking promises to the person I hope to become. I fully intend to replace whatever dreams I shattered when I was beating myself up. I have no idea where I learned "punching in" was a literal term. If I had known better, I would have called in sick in the head.

I accepted this position initially because I believed it came with the very best insurance plan. How could I fall to my death from the ground floor? Over the years, however, I've gotten increasingly familiar with the fine print of the benefits. Turns out, there are no benefits when the co-pay is your life.

I understand it's customary to give two weeks' notice, but I've only got two minutes, and in those minutes I will: 1) Fire my inner critic, or at least demote it to part time. 2) Assure my passions have the tools they need to unionize with my actions. 3) Sit naked on the photocopy machine so there are one hundred copies of my ass to kiss when I'm gone.

Though I suspect it won't bode well for acquiring a positive referral letter, it's important I state that I'm unwilling to train a replacement in this position. It is my suggestion that the job be eliminated altogether and that no future person take on the task.

If I can aid in the transition, please let me know.

Sincerely,

_____

EVERY TIME I EVER SAID I WANT TO DIE

—I meant I am willing to do anything to live.
Even leave this world forever.

> Even build a new home atop a nebula, stick a straw
> into a buried lake on Mars, get tipsy on anti-gravity
> and invent new constellations walking the lines
> between undiscovered stars.

> When god pulls me over and asks,
> Can you touch your nose? I could say,
> *What nose?*

> I'd be bodiless, a shadow in reverse,
> a patch of light made by the darkness
> I escaped.

The psychology manuals say no one really wants
to die. They want relief. They believe they will never
find it in this world. That belief could be right.
Or wrong.

One would have to stay to find out.
Friend, if you stay, at least we will be
together, and I have an extra straw.

> I could show you where the lakes on this planet
> are buried. How you do not need light-years
> to reach them. The dark years work too.
> Sometimes better. Sometimes grief
> is the fastest route to truth.

In addition to the straw,
I also have a slingshot that fires rock
bottoms directly at the sun until change
        spills from its golden pockets—

that's how I got my hands on this
summer afternoon. We can do anything
with it. Sunbathe or scream or forgive ourselves
everything, most especially the thread we could not
        convince to close our wounds.

If your wounds are still open, trust
they are doors to an answer,
and walk through.

What if we don't have to be healed
to be whole? There are holes in every inch
of the fabric that makes me who I am,

but pull the string on my back
and I'll say *I LOVE YOU* and mean it
whenever you want.

Come flood my home
with your eyes. I read that people scream
when they are in pain because screaming

actually lessens the pain—
anyone who asks you to hold your tongue
is asking you to hold the heaviest thing

in the galaxy. Forget them and remember you
can tell me anything about how hard it is
to stop flirting with your expiration date.

I understand being wooed by the finish line
of sadness. Infinity still sends me nudes
every day. I won't deny she looks amazing,

but I'm taken. My hand now promised
to writing every page of my story
except its end. Friend, you are

who taught me that a difficult life is not less
worth living than a gentle one. Joy is just easier
to carry than sorrow, and you could lift a city

from how long you've spent holding
what's been nearly impossible to hold.
This world needs those who know

how to do that. Those who can find
a tunnel with no light at the end
of it and hold it up like a telescope

to show that the darkness contains
many truths that can bring the light
to its knees. Grief astronomer,

adjust the lens, look close. Tell us
what you see.

INSTEAD OF DEPRESSION

try calling it hibernation.
Imagine the darkness is a cave
in which you will be nurtured
by doing absolutely nothing.
Hibernating animals don't even dream.
It's okay if you can't imagine
spring. Sleep through the alarm
of the world. Name your hopelessness
a quiet hollow, a place you go
to heal, a den you dug,
Sweetheart, instead
of a grave.

WHAT LOVE IS

She was on tour with me. She was on tour with me because I'd always preferred long distance, and I'd finally grown wise enough to know never to trust my preferences. Driving to a show one day we realized the venue where I'd be performing was only thirty minutes from her parents' home. I hadn't met them yet and wasn't sure I ever would, when out of nowhere they called and asked her to add them to the guest list. One tear sprinted down her cheek like it was running to a mailbox to open a letter it had been waiting for for seven hundred years. As for me, I vomited in my mouth and swallowed it like a champ.

It had been two decades since she came out. Two decades since her heart was something they had sincerely asked about. She grew up in the rural south. Five sisters and no telephone. Her father would have to sprint down the road to her grandpa's house to take a call about a job. Before hearing that, I hadn't known it was possible to work in oil and gas and not be rich, imagined him breaking his back on an oil rig in the Gulf Coast but really didn't have a clue what he actually did. She didn't have a clue what inspired them to want to come, but I suspected they'd heard the word poetry and thought, *That's gay in a good way.* Thought Walt Whitman with his cock still respectfully in the closet, stanza-ing about a shaft of summer grass, longing for only dogwood trees and lily pads. What I was certain of was that they weren't coming because they knew I'd ended my last show with a poem about how church yard sales are secretly the best places to buy dildos.

Right before showtime, she ran into the greenroom to tell me they'd arrived. Her smile, a jump rope stretched from one side of the room to the other, her breath leaping up and down in a giddy celebration: *They're here, they're here, they're actually here!* The two of us were like a team in a huddle right before the most important game of our queer lives, when a group walked in with a flyer for a protest, asking me to announce the details on the mic. It was a protest organized urgently to stop fracking in the state. *Yes, of course*, I said, tucking the flyer into a pocket with my set list. Then I saw the jump rope of my girlfriend's smile drop.

What's wrong? I asked. *Honey, fracking is why my dad has a job*, she said. *What? I can't not announce the protest*, I told her. *I know*, she said. *It would be a crime against my conscience.* She said, *I know*, heart big as the Titanic sinking to the bottom of the sea.

When I stepped on stage, her father was the first person I spotted. He was impossible to miss. A lumberjack in a forest of asymmetrical haircuts that looked even more asymmetrical next to her parents' straight backs, straight as telephone poles, and me—desperate for lines that could reach them.

Resting the flyer for the protest at my feet so I could announce it near the end, I told myself, *If you are going to be anything in the world tonight, you better be lightning. You better find something in you honest enough to strike them.*

For seventy-five minutes I spoke about nothing but love. How everything but *I love you* is small talk. How their daughter was the only person in the world sweet enough to always call me *honey*. How the first time we shared a bed she laid down with her arms tight at her side like a mummy, so terrified she was to love something and lose it again.

When the show was near its end, I looked down at the flyer and back at them. I'd say the moment lasted a lifetime, but no one lives that long. I could see the protest organizers in the audience waiting. I could see their faith in my politics and what they were sure was about to march from my lips, while I remembered the one tear that raced down my girlfriend's face, one tear with guts enough to hope, the look in her eye when she ran into the greenroom, belting, *They're here! They're here!*

.

I walked off the stage without saying a word against drilling the heart out of the earth. I walked up to the greenroom a hypocrite, a failed activist with my face in my hands on the couch, when her father burst through the door, his head nearly axing a hole through the ceiling, tears, like a giant's tears, covering his face. *I'm seventy-six years old*, he said, *and I just tonight figured out what love is.*

There is no moral of this story—there is only light and sadness. There is no moral of this story. It's just a moment in my life where I did something wrong, and the earth, who has never not known what love is, held me anyway.

HOMESICK: A PLEA FOR OUR PLANET

In the fifth grade, I won the science fair
with a project on climate change
that featured a papier-mâché ozone layer
with a giant hole through which a papier-mâché sun

burned the skin of a Barbie in a bikini
on a lawn chair, glaciers melting like the ice cubes
in her lemonade. It was 1987 in a town
that could have invented red hats,

but the school principal gave me
a gold ribbon and not a single bit of attitude
about my radical political stance
because neither he nor I knew

it was political. Science had not yet been
fully framed as *leftist propaganda*.
The president did not have a Twitter feed
starving the world of facts.

I spent that summer as I had every summer
before, racing through the forest behind my house
down the path my father called *the old logging road*
to a meadow thick with raspberry bushes

whose thorns were my very first heroes
because they did nothing with their life
but protect what was sweet.
Sundays I went to church but struggled

to call it *prayer* if it didn't leave grass stains
on my knees. Couldn't call it *truth*

if it didn't come with a dare to crawl
into the cave by the creek and stay there

until somebody counted all the way to one hundred.
I thought one hundred was the biggest number
there was. My mother absolutely blew my mind
the day she said, *One hundred and one.*

One hundred AND WHAT!?

Billionaires never grow out of doing that same math
with years. Can't conceive of counting past their own
lifespans. Believe the world ends the day they do.
Why are the keys to our future in the hands

of those who have the longest commutes
from their heads to their hearts? Whose greed
is the smog that keeps us from seeing
our own nature and the sweetness

we are here to protect? Do you know
sometimes when gathering nectar, bees fall asleep
in flowers? Do you know fish are so sensitive
snowflakes sound like fireworks when they land

on the water? Do you know sea otters hold hands
when they sleep so they don't drift apart?
Do you know whales will follow their injured friends
to shore, often taking their own lives

so as not to let a loved one be alone when he dies?
None of that is poetry. It is just the earth
being who she is in spite of us stamping
barcodes on the sea. In spite of us acting

like Edison invented daylight. Dawn
presses her blushing face to my window,
asks me if I know the records in my record collection
look like the insides of trees. Yes, I say,

there is nothing you have ever grown that isn't music.
You are the bamboo in Coltrane's saxophone reed.
The mulberries that fed the silkworms
that made the slippers for the ballet.

The pine that built the loom that wove the hemp
for Frida Kahlo's canvas. The roses that dyed her paint
hoping her brush could bleed for her body.
Who, more than the earth, has bled for us?

How do we not mold our hearts
after the first spruce tree who raised her hand
and begged to be cut into piano keys
so the elephants could keep their tusks?

The earth is the right side of history.
Is the canyon my friend ran to when no one else
he knew would echo his chosen name back
to him. Is the wind that wailed through 1956 Alabama

until the poplar trees carved themselves
into Dr. King's pulpit. Is the volcano that pours
the mercury into the thermometers held under
our tongues. The earth takes our temperature,

tells us when we are too hot,
even after we've spent decades denying
her fever. Our hands held to her burning forehead,
we insist she is fine while wildfires

turn redwoods to toothpicks, readying the teeth
of our apocalypse. She sends smoke signals
all the way from California to New York City—
ash falls from the sky. Do you know the mountains

of California used to look like they'd been set on fire
because they were so covered in monarch butterflies?
Do you know monarch butterflies migrate
three thousand miles using only the fuel

they stored as caterpillars in the cocoon?
We need so much less than we take.
We owe so much more than we give.
Squirrels plant thousands of trees every year

just from forgetting where they left
their acorns. If we aimed to be just half as good
as one of the earth's mistakes,
we could turn so much around.

Our living would be seed,
the future would have roots.
We would cast nothing from the garden
of itself. And we would make the thorns proud.

THE DAY PRINCE DIED

Everyone said you were his biggest fan.
You never did. You loved his music too much
to ever think no one could love it more than you.
You'd talk about his vocal range for days,
how he could start a note in one galaxy
and land it in another, how he discovered planets
with his songs. Planets where the lakes were lavender,
where the wind made the sound of a B-side hit
on vinyl, where everyone was six inches shorter
without shoes. In high school, you'd sneak out
of Iowa and drive through the dark to concerts
in his home at Paisley Park. By the time you were eighteen,
you knew more about his drummer than most people
know about themselves. When we met, you were saving
pennies to take red-eyes all over the continent
each time someone *in the know* said he'd be gracing
the stage of some tiny venue at 3AM in Chicago,
Minneapolis, L.A. I'd be at brunch in Colorado
when you'd call to say the show had just ended
after three encores that unraveled the axis
of Earth. I remember the sound of your sweat
through the phone on the fifty-sixth morning
you spent dancing to the dreams of a man who learned
to play twenty-seven instruments on his own.
The first birthday present I ever gave you
was a skateboard I'd painted with the sheet music
to Purple Rain. I didn't yet know true Prince fans
don't listen to Purple Rain. They listen to the silence
outside of vaults of unreleased songs—believing
the songs could save their lives and swearing
they'd rather die than press their ears to a single chorus
without his permission. Respect, I learned, was the first rule

to loving someone who would erase his own name
so it couldn't be sold. You said when you were near him
you wouldn't look at him too long. Taught your eyes
to hang back. Gave him more space than the moon.
Which is to say—he was your gravity.
He was much of the world's gravity.
He kept people here.

I don't remember why we couldn't get seats
together on the plane, but I do know I was exactly
sixteen rows behind you when the wheels touched
the ground, when we pulled up to the gate,
when the pilot's voice came over the speaker:
Folks, we've just received word
that Prince has died—

I'd crawled over the seat in front of me.
I was crawling over the next. I was almost fourteen
rows away when a mob of passengers, screaming
they were late for their destinations too, refused
to let me pass. I'd never in my life been so far away
from anywhere I needed to be.

When I found you in the terminal,
it was his pain, not yours, rushing from your eyes.
The thing about loving a stranger is you can guess,
but can never be sure, what they are privately surviving
on their journey to help others survive. *I'm just so grateful*
for him, you kept saying. *I'm just so grateful for him*. Mascara
running lines down your cheeks like he'd come back
to wipe your tears and left his guitar strings behind.

I was scheduled to go directly from the airport
to meet a friend who was grieving the death
of her mother. There was no way you would have let me

stay with you, but a whole universe exists in the moments
I spent weighing what to do, and I still visit
that universe on days I give up
on being an artist—

I go back to your bedroom in 2006 where you are
laying every album he ever made on the carpet.
Each record is a blueprint of you. In the corner now
is a man half-angel in skyscraper shoes. I watch him
watch you flip his vinyl to the B-side and drop the needle
into the groove. I watch him watch you watch my face
as his music hits my chest. I watch him close his eyes

and rest.

MY GENDER IS THE UNDOING OF GENDER

I wasn't always the pansy I am now. I used to have a perm,
and no one on Earth is tougher than a butch with a perm—
especially when wearing a backward baseball cap,
mascara, and a muscle shirt—wallet chain bouncing
off my quadricep. Military boots and a look in my eye
that said, *Give me a white flag and I'll use it for nothing*
but checking my oil and wiping my sweat. I drove
a Z24 Chevy. The muffler built to sound like a motorcycle
with a smoker's cough. I cried only in private and spent
not a single second alone. My best friends were barstools
and jocks. My shoulder blades sharp as my tongue,
which was in a perpetual state of *fuck off*—
but the day I got my first buzz cut, something
or everything changed. I looked in the mirror
and my tough relaxed. My body so at ease
my eyes could no longer hold the flood back.
Mascara raced off my face to water my fist—
which was no longer a fist but a carnation
in full bloom. Soon, I traded my car for a bicycle
with a basket, which I rode to the craft store
to buy thread to stitch fabric from the clothes
I was wearing into dolls I'd give as gifts
(too true to be believable, I know, but it is).
At the bar, Budweiser in hand, my pinky finger
ballerina'd into the air. I looked like a princess
sipping tea. About to chase my finger back inside,
I sung, *Good god, Andrew, let that sweet child*
run free.   Andrew—it was the first time
I'd said it out loud—and I'd say more now
but it's all quite simple: I became this me
so I could finally be the fairy I always was.
I cut my hair and grew out my feelings

instead. If someday I have a mustache,
I know I'll be comfortable wearing a dress.
And if I ever have a beard, I'm certain
              I'll be the prettiest girl I've ever been.

SPELLING BEE WITHOUT STINGER

I love myself
is often spelled
g-o-o-d-b-y-e

THE NIGHT SHIFT

They offer me the job on the spot,
citing my previous work in construction
which I'd almost left off my résumé,
figuring jackhammers, drill bits,
and wrenches are not tools one can use
working at an at-risk-youth home for girls.
There's a lot here falling apart, the house
psychologist says, after a clothesline
of a girl busts into our interview and falls
to the floor, tearing her baby blue press-on
nails through the carpet. Her mother missed
visiting day for the third week in a row.
The creases of the girl's worn dress
are ironed so perfectly I know that, this week,
she was certain her mother would come.
I'm in the darkest year of my twenties
and applied for the night shift
in an attempt to trick myself into believing
that sleeping through the day was healthy.
From 10PM until 8AM, my job is to walk
the hallways where the girls sleep and shine
a tiny flashlight as softly as possible
into each bunk every twenty minutes,
all night long. It is an invasion of privacy
I can only stomach when recalling
the kindness of the social worker's eyes
when she walked me through my training.
*Many of these girls are not wanted
by their families, and there are few things
that make it harder to want to stay alive,*
she said, removing an item I had never
considered someone could hurt

themselves with from a girl's closet.
It was only one item on a long list
of things I am being paid to memorize
and will spend the years ahead of me
trying to forget. The more I know the girls,
the harder the job becomes.
Bracing for the blood of a stranger
is one hell, but the terror is multiplied
by my every bitten nail when that stranger
is a girl who has told me all her life's stories
except for the one I heard in the staff meeting
and could not believe any human could live through.
For years to come, nothing will have the potential
to devastate me more than listening to a child try
to make her life sound easier than it is.
A month into the job, I can't look at any of the girls
without seeing my baby sister's face
the first time someone hurt her on purpose.
It wasn't my sister's grief so much as her shock

that stuck with me. None of these girls
are shocked by the hurt that hunts them—
they expect the blade of this life
to keep cutting and ask it to whittle
them into someone too sharp to touch.
I've never in my life known a relief
like the one that finds me the instant their alarms
start screaming in the morning. It's the sound
of teenagers having lived through the night.
I make a pot of coffee and listen to them punch
their snooze buttons until they file into the office
to sign out pink razors, one at a time. Jenny
is always up first. My job is to stand outside
the closed bathroom door and request
a voice check-in every two minutes.

She would hate me for this if how much I despise
doing it was any less clear. Showers are for peace,
not for being reminded you can't be trusted
not to bury yourself in six feet of dirt
while getting yourself clean. I've had many jobs
before this one and will have many after, but this
is where I learn one of the most vital lessons:
if your own story is one you aren't sure
you can survive, remove whatever sharpness
you can from another person's life.

Two minutes have passed.

Jenny, check in with me, I say, checking
my watch outside the bathroom door.
Whatever song she was singing
went silent, and all I can hear
is the water slapping the drain.

Two minutes and thirty seconds have passed.

Jenny, check in with me,
I say again, moving my ear closer
toward the door and feeling
my pulse begin to knock
its way out of my chest.

Three minutes have passed.

Jenny, check in . . .

    —I'm okay, Andrea, she says,
just as my hand reaches for the knob.

Don't do that again or I'll kill you! I yell.

Jenny laughs. The line
of girls behind me in the hallway
laughs with her.

Then Jenny starts singing again.
And after some time,
I do too.

LOVE ME TO LIFE

I got sick in 2003, and as much as I tried, illness was a relationship I could never manage to leave. In spite of seeing every doctor in Colorado, I could not divorce my body from its pain. In 2010, I woke up in a scream that lasted eight months. A Charley horse bucking through my blood. I didn't believe I could live through it for half an hour, then half a year passed and it was still nowhere close to tamed. I struggled to walk from my bed to the bathroom, left my house for nothing but my shows. That I didn't just cancel what would have been healthy to cancel was a side effect of both shame and having been raised proudly working class by a father who hated having a heart attack less than he hated having to call in sick because of it. To make it through my tour, I wore an eight-year-old's pink sequin dance leotard hidden beneath my clothes for every reading—a makeshift compression suit to ease the pain bought at a dance store beside a venue on a night I knew it would be as easy for me to stand up on stage for sixty minutes as it would for me to win the Olympics. Every week a new doctor would ask my symptoms. I'd always answer, *My blood feels like crushed glass.* I had no other way to explain it. They had no idea what to do. Once during a layover in Chicago, my legs at that point atrophied to toothpicks, it took me ninety minutes to walk from one gate to the next. By the time I boarded, I felt so close to death I was certain the plane would be my casket, so right before takeoff I lost it—wailing like an ambulance in the aisle of United 685 until the plane stopped on the runway and turned around to feed me to the arms of medics. Needless to say, it wasn't the sexiest moment of my life. Though do I believe the flight attendants still dream about me—I guarantee it's not because they think I'm freaky in a good way. Some months later I finally got diagnosed with chronic Lyme disease, started a pantry of meds and was improving, but when I hit a roadblock in healing, I began a weekly treatment where essentially they'd take out my blood, clean it, and put it back in. During my first appointment, I almost vomited seeing that my blood was the color of tar and a similar texture. The doctor said it was common with the disease, but it gave me the willies watching something come out of my veins that looked like it had come from a gutter. One week, noticing my blood had worsened after I'd gotten into an argument with a friend, I became obsessed with what I might be able to do on my own to turn my blood red. Before every weekly appointment I'd experiment. What happens to the color when I meditate? What happens when I do yoga? What happens if I put nothing in my body but seaweed, dandelion leaves, and juiced kale? What happens if I bathe in salted crystals while chanting into my root chakra while breathing sage into the lungs of a cloud shaped like Mother Mary admitting some sexy devil swallowed her holy cherry? Some of my experiments actually helped brighten my blood a bit but not so much that I wasn't losing faith and, sunk by despair, I spent an entire long weekend doing nothing but drinking and fucking. Mostly fucking—a woman I'd adored for years but had only recently had the courage to ask out, or ask in, since I still could rarely go out. She stayed with me for three days and I don't remember a minute where I didn't feel like a country farm boy getting gratefully ruined in the bed of his daddy's truck. My body, a graffitied confession booth turned inside out for this woman's truth. At one point a pig walked over from the neighbor's field, pressed his snout to the door, and fogged up the glass watching us get dirty on a bean bag on the living room floor. We stopped as soon as we saw the pig, shooed the kinky angel back to his home, and kept going. Walking into my appointment on Monday morning, I was so terrified of the dark I knew they'd find inside of me, I slammed my eyes closed when the doctor slid the needle into my arm. They were still shut when he belted, *Jesus Christ!* I opened my eyes and my blood

was so bright. It was the color
of pomegranate seeds, of wild strawberries,
of ladybugs in love. It was the color of falling
autumn maple leaves, the part of the sunset
you cannot believe is real. My blood
was the color of the lipstick she left
on my collarbone, the color of her fingernails
dug into my hips, the color of my blushing
when she first told me to feel her up

and I accidentally started unbuttoning
her pants—I do not have a clue
how I managed to live almost four decades
without knowing *feel me up* means *touch my boobs*—

but I know it now. I know it now, just like I know my blood
is red, when it's red, at least partially because of love.

Because of what holds me to the light. What touches me
to the core. What shined me like a ruby and wore me

around her neck. You can die from a broken heart.
I've watched it happen. I've watched someone's body

follow a loved one's body to the other side.
It was the hardest thing I've ever witnessed in my life,

but it was the softest, too, one heart stopping
to tell another heart, *I'm coming with you.*

You can die from a broken heart,
but the opposite is also true.

LOVE LETTER TO THE TICK THAT GOT ME SICK

Unlike almost anything else,
the tiniest ones are the most dangerous.

The doctor said you were probably no bigger
than a poppy seed when you leapt
from a birch tree and landed triumphant

in the always messy nest of my hair.
A few days later, bloated on my once-good blood,

you likely escaped down the shower drain,
billowed in a sudsy heaven of Suave shampoo
(me having been too much inside of my head

to have noticed you on top of it).
I'd flown home to the woods of Maine

to spend the summer caring
for my eight-month-old niece,
while my still-teenage sister

was a million miles away
in a trailer on the other side of town,

men twice her age offering needles
for her arm so she could sew herself
backward, unmake her own life

one fix at a time. All day
my niece and I would sit beneath the pines

that canopied my parents' home
that my family had built two years prior
with a second shipment of lumber—

the first shipment stolen in the middle of the night
by a truck big enough to lug an entire home's

worth of cedar. *Had to be an 18-wheeler.*
That's what those drugs will do. Have a sweet kid
steal the roof over her parent's heads

before it's even built. In every photo
from that summer, my niece is wearing

a hat. A short-billed train conductor cap
I'd coaxed from the hands of my best friend
when she'd dropped me at the airport in Denver.

Please, I begged. *It will help me*
not lose my mind.

Each morning, as soon as the sun
opened the curtains of the room
my niece and I shared, I'd carry her

outside toward the only entertainment
for a hundred miles: a chubby-cheeked squirrel

eating pinecones like corn on the cob.
A tree frog with its feet suction-cupped
to the living room window that had been too clean

for the robin to see. How strange
it was then, to watch a thing be killed

by something being *too clean*.
Throughout the summer, whenever the nest
of baby wrens screamed with excitement

over their mother's return, I'd hold my niece
tighter. What grief looked like on a baby,

I knew I wasn't strong enough to see.
To distract her, I'd rip the hat off my head
and place it on hers, which would lodge a smile

across her holy pudgy face.
She looks like a dinner roll with eyes,

I'd holler to my mother, then snap
a photo to send to my sister, praying
the breadcrumb trail of cuteness would lead her home.

There are a thousand places you could have found me,
Poppy Seed, but I like to think this was when—

when I took the hat off my head
and placed it on hers. I like to think you waited
until you saw her head was covered

to throw yourself from that tree,
knowing your body was a tiny grenade,

and soldiers who don't want to be soldiers
have control over almost nothing
except for their aim.

Fourteen years have passed since then.
My sister is sober and happy and a porch light

wherever she goes.
My niece is the tallest kid in her class
in every way there is to grow.

Together they take photographs
that are breadcrumbs that lead me home,

and when I visit, I bring you with me
in every muscle and bone.
You are my blood now.

Which is another word for *family*—
which is the least tiny gift

my life has known.

AFTER THE BREAK-UP, OUR TANDEM BIKE SPEAKS:

To say it was anyone's fault
would be to misunderstand

the headwind that every love faces.
How quickly a halo can bust a hole
and go flat. One rock

bottom and there is nothing left
but something to be replaced.

Call it jealousy, but couldn't
it also be called faith? To believe
there is always something

better than you out there?
People, without knowing, choose

the hardest gears. Harder and harder
until they stop moving forward.
Stop moving forward and it's impossible

not to crash. I know I'm not built
to believe in anything but forever.

I know what I call freedom,
others call a chain. It's true that everything
about me says, *Please stay together—*

you can say it's just how I was made.
But I'm certain it's more about what I've seen,

and most people don't leave
because the pedals have turned into love-me-
nots—that's just how they spin

the story to not have to grieve
a more impossible thing: that history

didn't stay in its lane. That the tiniest dents
rusted so much away they simply stopped
knowing how to hold each other

tighter than they could
hold the brakes.

        I understand that I am nothing without them.
        I understand that I am something that is nothing

        without love. But what in this world
        would I rather be than something

        that is nothing without love?
        It's worth the rest of my days

        covered in dust.

NEIGHBORS

Debbie O'Doyle hated me. She couldn't help it.
The dreadlocked white boys who'd rented the house
before me spent their tuition money turning the basement
into a psychedelic farm, and retirees with plastic deer
lawn ornaments rarely enjoy being woken up at 3AM
by flower-crowned sorority girls riding their plastic fawn
through the center of a previously respectable street.

After three years of pressing binoculars to her window,
writing down the license plate numbers of every Jeep Wrangler
with an *I'M A FUNGI* bumper sticker, Debbie finally convinced
the cops to bust the door down and harvest the fun guys
(which was bountiful for me only because the lock
wasn't properly fixed and the landlord was forced to knock
$100 off my first month's rent).

Debbie O'Doyle didn't see me as an upgrade to the neighborhood,
I suspect, because I had nothing to show for myself on move-in day
except a box of tattered books, an old bicycle, and a couch
I'd found on the curb a block away which she'd seen me roll
on two skateboards to the front door, tattooed and shoeless,
singing a folk song with the F-word in the chorus.

Here's another one come to grow mushrooms
in a turd pile under the house, she must have thought,
having no way of knowing I wouldn't
dream of growing psychedelics in my home.

I'd do what everyone else does and buy them from a friend
who grows them in *his* home, and I certainly wouldn't stoop
to eating the god-buttons in the concrete hell of the city

when there were real live deer waiting for me to ride them
in the forest just two miles away.

For an entire year Debbie O'Doyle watched me
like a detective hawk, screeching as if *I* were the one
with the claws and she were the one with the puncture wounds
in the ever-bleeding skull of her solitude.

Andrea! That BBQ of yours
better be over by 9PM sharp!

Andrea! Your dandelions
aren't going to weed themselves!

Andrea! If you try to pretend that roof
is a party deck one more time . . . !

Andrea. Andrea. Andrea!

I had no idea how she knew my name.
Introductions don't happen from opposite sides of a street,
and Debbie refused to cross the road. Spent the entirety
of her days pacing the end of her driveway, begging me
to take one step out of the house so she could belt, *Andrea!*
Your theater friends stole my ornamental toad!

The only thing I ever remember speaking to Debbie O'Doyle
was, *They aren't theater friends! They are poet friends!*
And they would never in a million years steal
your plastic lawn toad!

But I knew they stole her toad, of course, and this is where
our relationship was and where I knew it would remain
when I woke up that September morning to my landline ringing

like a siren, my friend through the wire, crying,
Turn on the TV! Turn on the TV!

It was 2001. Not only did I not have a TV,
I didn't have the internet, a cell phone, or a car—so shoeless
and still in my pajamas, I did the unthinkable and ran
across the street to pound on Debbie's door.

She was so unsurprised
to see me on her porch,

I knew the world
had changed.

We sat on opposite ends
of her sofa as a cloud

of black smoke screamed
from the top of the North Tower.

I wanted to turn my eyes
from the screen

but knew what I couldn't
see was worse—the people

on the floors above the ones
on fire, calling home

and getting a machine.
And then, what it is

for a mother to stare
down a plane, nose to nose.

The newscaster spotted something
that stole his capacity to speak

and Debbie and I
moved closer on the couch.

Was it right then
that she understood

the neighbors before me
and their desperation

to grow another world?
Was it right then

that I asked her
her name?

NOTE TO THE STRANGER SIX FEET AWAY:

There was never not a bridge from your chest to mine. My heartbeat was always the sound of your feet walking toward me. I can't believe how many years I lived without knowing the air you were breathing out was the air I was breathing in. Forgive me for not saying *thank you* before our lungs had reason to hide. Do you pray more now than you used to? I pray all the time. I pray to the Big Bang and to the Tiny Bang and to the bangs we'll all have to cut ourselves so we can see what beauty can only be seen from six feet away. A giraffe's neck is six feet long. A decade from now, will I remember the week I spent wondering if I could hug a giraffe's torso and not get sick if the giraffe coughed? I don't want to forget anything about this. Especially not how it feels to worry about everyone I love at the same time—so much of the world had been doing that already.

If every heart-worthy novelist weeps for days before killing off a beloved character, god must have spent centuries sobbing before pressing a pen to the page of this year.

GOOD GRIEF

Let your
heart break

so your spirit
doesn't.

THE CALL, OPTION 1

*I pay seventeen dollars online to track down the phone number
of the man who sexually assaulted me, and my friend asks, "What
do you plan to say?"*

I'll tell him I know he lost
all his money gambling
and was forced

to sell the building
where he did what he did.
I'll tell him karma is a hell

of a feminist.
I'll tell him my silence
was his worst bet.

I'll tell him I'm watching
him through the bullet hole
he left in my childhood,

and if he comes within
two hundred miles
of a child's trust, my body

will start bleeding his name
all over Main Street in his middle-
of-somewhere town.

I'll tell him
he's the middle of nowhere:
a man with no stop

lights, the kind of place kids grow up
desperate to escape. I'll tell him
as soon as I got out,

I imagined him sanding off
his fingerprints, the guilt
filing him down to half his size.

When I met him,
he was the biggest man
in town, had set records

in the deadlift, was as old
as my father. I weighed
ninety-six pounds, was still

spending sleepovers practicing
how to kiss. I'll tell him how big
I am now. So big

I could make his address
the title of my next book,
and yes, I think he asked for it.

Asked me to play hangman
with his name on the local news,
asked me to spray paint *ME TOO*

across his pickup truck
and say, *I dare you*
to compare property damage

with someone you made property.
With someone whose puberty
you mutilated.

I'll say, *Trauma*
is a pretty word for how to die
every day of the year,

but my voice is alive
and right now it is the only justice
system I trust

to ensure men like you
understand the law
of gravity, understand

you will always be held down
by what you held down.
There is no such thing as rising

from someone else's ashes.
No man's spirit escapes the hell
he denies putting a child through,

which is to say, I am the only one
out of the two of us who survived
you, and I survived you

so beautifully. Even on my worst days,
my scars are the backroads
where kids sneak out their windows

and drive through the night
to hear poetry. I am so much
of who I dreamed I'd be

when I grew up, and what
does the boy you once were
think of the man you became?

A man running
from his own name.
A man who must wake

fifty times a night, terrified
the truth is somewhere breaking
from its chains and racing

for the world's ear.
When the truth gets there, will you try
to tell your friends I wanted it?

Will you try to tell your wife
how old of a soul I was?
At *thirteen*? At thirteen,

I had the youngest soul
in the universe.
I was so brand new

I thought reincarnation
was a flower I would wear
on my wrist

if someday someone asked me
to the ninth-grade dance.
I'd stand in my full-length mirror

and practice not blushing
when a slow song came on.
That's how old I was.
That's the kind of man you were.
The kind of man who makes children
grow up and search

for your phone number,
our bodies riddled with the wish
that all the records will say:
No one by that name exists.

THE CALL, OPTION 2

I pay seventeen dollars online to track down the phone number of the man who sexually assaulted me, and my friend asks, "What do you plan to say?"

There is a world in which you did not touch me.
A world in which you thought about touching me
and were so nightmared by your own mind
you climbed inside your skull and bloodied your knees

crawling across the tundra of your history,
turning over every rock to chase out every worm
that might trick you into believing anything
could be cut in half and keep living.

There is a world in which you saw
how easily you could become an ax
splitting the personalities of children,
so swore your fingerprints

would be like the rings of trees, that your growth
could be counted on. In this world you have
groomed no one, and I am made of flyaways—
gleefully unclipped, wholly uncombed through,

braiding myself around a song, certain
I've invented dancing. Look at me
still calling you a hero. You built my trust
and never became the quake of earth

that shattered my foundation. Look at you
mothering your own nature, calling yourself home
at the first sign of dark. In this world you might
still be poor but not where it counts.

You might have still lost all your money,
but look at what you saved: Me
and Her and Her and Her and Her and Her
and the child you once were—how proud

he is to see who he's become. In this world
you still have secrets, but they are like my father's
secrets. The ones he doesn't know I know.
The ones my grandma told me: how he stayed

home nearly every weekend of high school
to keep my grandfather's drunken fist from the glass
of her jaw, how good my father was at pretending
he didn't love the movies, hadn't saved

all summer to buy a secondhand suit
for his first school dance. There is a world
in which you, too, only lie to save someone's life,
a world where you still live a stone's throw

from Canada but walk the river's shore never plotting
how you'd swim to freedom, never practicing
the backstroke of denial, never hoping I drowned
the letters you wrote me when I was graduating

eighth grade and you were forty and marrying
someone you said would never be your type.
The first time I called, your wife answered
the phone. I hung up, not strong enough

to be like you—to throw a brick through
a woman's chest and have no doubts about it
being the right move, but there is a world
in which the truth is as soft as the pillow

that holds your wife's head when she dreams
about the day you met. In this world you wake up
before she does, make her coffee, read her horoscope
and forget to read your own. Where you stand behind her

when she looks in the mirror, tell her she's grown
more gorgeous every one of her sixty-seven years,
how you feel like the richest man in town
with your hands in the silver

of her hair. In this world I celebrate the news
of you having a daughter, a granddaughter, a niece.
In this world I don't panic when I see a pink tricycle
in your neighbor's driveway

as I'm driving to meet friends at the riverfront,
my hometown still a home you never haunted.
I roll the window down, holler your name
into the autumn air. You look up

from raking a pile of golden leaves, smile
and wave back to me. Can you see it?
I know you can. Everyone can
see who they were supposed to be.

It's the readiest grief in the world.

WHAT CAN'T BE TAKEN

Trauma was not being
able to get the hands
of the clock off me.

Healing was learning
no one has ever laid a fingerprint
on the part of me that's infinite.

THE TEST OF TIME

I am twenty years old and my mother has just been diagnosed
with a disease that is beginning to paralyze her.

She holds my hand on the couch and tells me
the disease is hereditary. Runs through family trees

until no one runs again. With the diagnosis, she finally knows
why her favorite aunt spent the second half of her life

in a wheelchair. Why her father's gait began to change
before he died too young for his doctor to uncover the reason.

I'm twenty years old and there is a test I can take
to find out if the disease has been coded in my DNA,

if I'll be able to do the two-step in my genes
on a dance floor two decades from now.

The test is a psychic. A crystal ball. A tarot reading
from the edge of a cliff from which I may or may not fall.

I'm twenty years old and I've always been afraid
of the Ouija board. When someone asks how I will die,

my fingers dive off the board and into my pockets
like, *Can't we please let god keep her secrets?*

My whole life I've known my mother
as the town walker. Ever since my bike had training wheels,

I've been riding beside her every night at dusk.
She walks for miles, a smile on her face

that turns on the porch light of every house
she passes. I don't burden her

with asking what she would do,
if she would have wanted to know she'd hit forty

and forty would hit her back, a baseball bat to the knees,
her life as she knew it giving out beneath her.

I'm twenty years old and I haven't met
any of my disabled friends yet,

which means I still believe what the world has taught me
to believe—that life will not take my breath away

unless it's taking my breath away at the summit
of Kilimanjaro, or atop the crest of a sixty-foot

skateboard ramp on the Pacific Coast.
I don't yet know Natalie, who will be sipping whiskey

at the end of my bed when she tells me she would not choose
the sudden disappearance of her cerebral palsy,

that the hard drive of her mind would crash
if she woke up tomorrow and could cartwheel

the beach, if suddenly it took her less than thirty minutes
to lace her winter boots. When Natalie says this, I wake up

to a truth—that I've not wanted my fortune told
because I've not wanted to know

that my fortune will be mostly change.
So much change. I'm twenty years old

and don't know that what I'm most afraid of
is change, which is the only promise

this life can keep, and aside from my DNA,
there is no test I can take to find out the rest of it,

or the unrest of it, how there will be years I'll know
so much bitterness my heart will stop walking

its talk. Lovers will point to my chest
and say, *You can't feel anything, can you?*

I'm twenty years old and don't know who I am
going to lose because of the ways I'm going to stay

the same, then later because of the ways I'm going
to change too much. I mean, my god is gonna change.

My pronouns are gonna change. My body is gonna change
not because of my DNA but because a tick is gonna bite me

and that little monster is gonna mess with my life
more than a parade of homophobes could ever dream of,

but love will still throw me over her shoulder and carry me up
every story I've ever told myself so I can see what's true,

and what's true is I can't always tell the difference
between my gifts and my tragedies. What I've lost

in health I've gained in access to my own empathy.
So when I wish to not be sick, I'm not absolutely certain

I'd be happier if that wish came true, and the same goes
for what muzzled me, what held me down and shut me up,

what locked my voice box is also what taught me
how to carve keys from poetry, and now my words

are so good at coming to my own rescue,
fire trucks pull over to let my voice through.

Hold my tongue and I promise my teeth
will find a way to tell you, *If I'd been born without lifelines,*

I would have written them myself, 'cause I am writing this
at the exact age my mother was when she first got symptoms,

and just like everyone else I have no clue
what tomorrow will sing, or scream, what I will feel

or what I won't. I wake up every morning and see
if I can still wiggle my toes, and I dance

in my pajamas before I brush my teeth, and I pray
to a different god every single day because I pray to me,

and sometimes I'm clear and sometimes I'm scattered
as the ashes of my friends who were still alive last year,

but there is a test we can all take to find out the future.
It's called the test of time. And what you do is you live

until you die. And you refuse to let the hands of your clock
curl into fists to fight the lessons off. Even if the lessons

are brutally hard. In all my softest dreams my mother
can still walk. And I am pedaling my bicycle beside her.

ALIENS EXPLAIN WHY THEY ARE VISITING EARTH

Because your leaders
    move their fingers
over the buttons of bombs

    as if they are piano keys.
As if they could make a symphony
    of playing chords around

your children's necks.
    Because if the heart
of the earth is in Arizona,

the Grand Canyon is proof
    of how badly it is breaking.
Because we want to pace

    your border towns and teach
families the physics of walking
    through walls.

    Because we don't
understand why you believe hell
    is beneath you.

    Also—because we want to
hear old men play Vivaldi
    in subway stations in Queens.

    Because we want to watch
skateboarders in Berlin
    carve the streets

into statues of themselves.
        Because we know
kids in New Orleans

        glue bottle caps to the soles
of their shoes and tap dance
        in Jackson Square.

Because we've never
        seen anything like that anywhere.
We have so many questions.

        Why do you fly saucers
from the coffee table into the living
        room wall and insist your sadness

doesn't exist? How did you come to believe
        that hating yourself would protect you
from other people's hate? What

        do you mean when you say
your hearts *melt*? Are they like glaciers?
        Can one person die and drown

the whole world?
        Is that what Jesus did
when he meant to do the opposite?

We are visiting from so far away
        we thought it was the furthest
one could go until we saw the distance

        between two lovers
who had been sharing the same bed
        for four decades. We are trying

to make sense of the light-years
        it takes to get from one side
of a dinner table to another

        when you have buried someone
in the dirt you think they have
        on you. To be human, it seems,

is to know your true self
        only as well as you know
a galaxy you've never been to.

We came here to help you
        get there.

CONSTELLATIONS REARRANGE THEMSELVES INTO A PROTEST SIGN

Every uprising has
the universe
on their side.

That's not a horizon.
That's the earth
drawing the line.

CLIMATE CHANGE

You've been driving in circles all day
on the backroads through the farmlands
where everything is so close to the earth
the silos look like skyscrapers.
It's been weeks since the first breath
of winter, and the geese are just beginning
to make their long trip south. They fly
in a perfect > but they do not think
what is ahead of them is greater or less than
what is behind them. That, you are certain,
is the definition of peace. But you have not known
peace in many months, since the day
your love's shoulder turned cold.
You were standing in the kitchen the first time
you noticed the temperature dropping. A storm front
rolled across her face. Ice forming in her once-warm tone.
You had no idea what was happening.
It was a season you had never seen.
Everything before then—summer. Years of her
grabbing your hand and pulling you toward
a teal August sea. Looking back, you think
if you'd had just one week of autumn, if
you'd seen even a single leaf turn
from green to red, you might have been
prepared. Might have even thought it natural.
Everything you know about climate change
insists the sudden shifts are what's most dangerous.
It was eighty degrees one day and below freezing
the next. You turn onto Maple Bridge Road
just as another flock of geese lands on a half-frozen lake.
Geese can migrate 1,200 miles in a single day.
If you drove through the night, you could too.

It's not a thought but an instinct. A knowing
that you aren't built to survive this kind of cold.
Where will you go? a friend on the phone asks.
Somewhere warm, you say, and if it were years
earlier, you know that somewhere would be
a someone. But you're done making vacations
out of people. You want a permanent home.
You want decades of her teasing you for folding
her sundresses terribly. Geese, unlike many birds,
do not fly south at the first cold breeze. They wait
until they are nearly buried by the blizzard. They stay
until they can't find one last edible seed. That day
in the kitchen when the ponds of her eyes froze,
you started skating a figure 8 across them, over
and over, trying to etch infinity back into what she saw
when she looked at you. But visibility is drastically reduced
in a storm, and it has not stopped snowing, so staying
may no longer be an option. But before you go,
remember the weather almost never shifts
this suddenly by itself. You've scoured the soil
for her carbon footprint a thousand times,
but have you scoured it for yours? Not to go
looking for shame but to know your own
impact. And can you do that without deciding
you are a poison in the air? Before you leave,
put those questions on the map. Love yourself
enough to go there.

WELLNESS CHECK

In any moment,
on any given day,
I can measure
my wellness
by this question:

Is my attention on loving,
or is my attention on
        who isn't loving me?

MY GIRLFRIEND'S KARAOKE SONG

I've been told as a kid she never stopped singing
just in case there was a talent scout in line behind her
at the bagel shop, or walking past her in the mall,
or listening from the adjacent dressing room

while she tried on school clothes
at Target in the third grade.
I've seen photographs of the concerts
she put on in nursing homes

with her Spice Girls cover band.
I know the chocolate pudding cups
in the hands of her audience members
couldn't keep her from taking it

so seriously she lost friends in the process,
tiny girls who couldn't reach the high notes
of her expectations, so I'm not surprised
to find myself sitting alone

at the karaoke bar eating French fries
while she practices her song
in the restroom stall, the same song
she's been singing all week

in the shower, in the ice cream aisle
at the grocery store, on our long drive home
from puppy training class, or climbing the stairs
to couples therapy where I tell our therapist

that I believe she starts arguments
just so I'll storm out of the house
and leave her alone with the living room
acoustics. Since she left me here,

I've heard a drunk college boy sing
Like a Virgin, the irony no doubt intended
to prove him very unlike a virgin. I've heard
a woman in a neck brace sing Whitney Houston

while snapping bubble gum
through the instrumental bridge.
I've watched a man in a half-shirt sing *With a Little
Help from My Friends* exactly like Joe Cocker

might have if he'd had a hard time
making friends. Everything about the place
takes me back to where I come from, a small town
where dreams never come true,

so nobody ever stops dreaming.
A place where you are loved
not for how well you sing
but for your willingness

to pick a song everyone will want
to sing with you. My girl isn't exactly
from another world, but she's an out-of-towner
in the sense that I'm terrified

the world will end if she can't
hear a pin drop when she sings
You Were Meant for Me,
which is actually sung

in a very difficult key—E minor,
with a moderate, swinging tempo
of 114 beats per minute. If she doesn't
nail it at the beginning,

it will be nearly impossible
to come back from. The only way
she won't be doomed is if she jumps
an octave right before the first words

of the chorus, which are, *Dreams*
last so long—and yes, they do.
Even after they're gone.
But dreams are never really gone

if someone's dreaming with you.
You wanna know what my girl says
to every artist she knows? She says,
I'm rooting for you.

So I know more about Jewel's music
than is probably sane to know, sitting here
listening to a bachelorette rap Eminem
over the bartender screaming, *Douglas!*

Come get your chicken wings!
As I check over my shoulder for talent
scouts and wait for my girl
        to sing.

WHAT YOU WISH YOU'D SAID TO THE HIGH SCHOOL GUIDANCE COUNSELOR

I don't aim to be a person of note.
I aim to be a person of whole journals
filled with stories about hitchhiking
the Atlantic coast.

Being born took courage, sir.

I'm not gonna waste the daylight
trying to darken seven-hundred tiny
circles on a test just right. How on earth
is that anything close to an answer?

Everybody wants straight A's.
Give me some gay A's to work for.*
You're talking to someone
whose imaginary friends were bullies.

You're talking to someone who drank
from the fountain after Connie McGary
drank from the fountain and thought
it might be my only real kiss.

You're talking to someone
who wore a lifejacket to the baptism
because I knew—I knew
what they were trying to do.

---

* My girlfriend tried to get me to edit this line out of the poem.
   Should I have listened to her?
   O yes
   O no

I'm not looking for a degree.
I'm looking for eighty-six degrees
in June and whatever will keep
my snowboard humming through December.
I come from a long line of people
who never heard of *cutting edge*.
They're mending-edge. My grandma Izzy,
a nurse. My grandma Faye, a seamstress,

and you think I'm gonna show up
to this life believing it's someone else's job
to do the fixing? If living gets lonely,
I'll get a job as a toll booth worker

and make thirty new friends
a minute. You got something better
than that to offer me? You got something
sweeter than the honey I shimmied

from the hive myself? You got a plan
for my life richer than the one where I pick
a lucky penny up and ask some song
of a woman to marry me for my money?

I don't think so, sir.
I really really really don't think so.

WHAT SUCKS ABOUT THE AFTERLIFE

On Earth, everyone loved butterflies,
but I trusted the caterpillars more.
I trusted the ones who knew

they were not done growing.
On Earth, I was a work in progress,
was comforted in the knowing

that I had a million mistakes still in me
to learn from. I changed my mind
more often than I changed my socks,

and whenever I was criticized
for mismatched thoughts, I'd say,
Who wants to be today

who they were yesterday?
Becoming was how I prayed.
But here—I am past the finish line:

I have a heart of gold,
and I never have to dig for it.
I couldn't do anything wrong if I tried,
and trust me, I try, but

I get hot-headed, and my rage
toasts the marshmallow on an angel's
celestial s'mores. I lose my temper and find it
in the halo lost-and-found box.

Lies won't let me tell them.
They handed me a sticker
that said *My Name Is* and I wrote
Everyone by accident. I can't remember

what selfishness is. Yesterday I said
something angry about an ex, and a quarter
of my tastebuds jumped off my tongue.
I've known nothing

of bitterness since.
Right before I died, I thought,
*In the afterlife, I'll apply for a job
at a mistake factory. They'll be awed*

by my résumé. If anything, I'm overqualified.
But there's no place where they make
mistakes here. Everyone is flawless.
Everyone's blunders are photoshopped

right off their lives before
they even happen. Is this heaven
or hell? I can't tell. I looked
that famous carpenter up

in the phone book, but his number
wasn't listed, and I need to ask him
where to find the wood to build
some missteps. I'm not about to spend

eternity burning in the lie that holy
and *perfect* are the same thing.
Do you understand?

A promised land
is not a promised land
if I can't keep learning.

HOW THE WORST DAY OF MY LIFE
BECAME THE BEST

When you are trapped in a nightmare, your motivation
to awaken will be so much greater than that of someone
caught up in a relatively pleasant dream. —Eckhart Tolle

When I realized the storm
      was inevitable, I made it
            my medicine.

Took two snowflakes
      on the tongue in the morning,
            two snowflakes on the tongue
            by noon.

There were no side effects.
      Only sound effects. Reverb
            added to my lifespan,
                an echo that asked—

What part of your life's record is skipping?

What wound is on repeat?

Have you done everything
you can to break
out of that

groove?

By nighttime, I was intimate
    with the difference
        between tying my laces
            and tuning the string section

        of my shoes, made a symphony of walking
            away from everything that did not
            want my life
                        to sing.

Felt a love for myself so consistent
    metronomes tried to copyright
        my heartbeat.

Finally understood I am the conductor
    of my own life and will be even after I die.
        I, like the trees, will decide what I become:

        porch swing?

                Church pew?

            An envelope that must be licked
                to be closed?

    Kinky choice, but
        I didn't close.

        I opened
            and   opened

until I could imagine the pain
was the sensation of my spirit
not breaking,

that my mind was a parachute
that could always open
in time,
that I could wear my heart
on my sleeve and never grow
out of that shirt.

That every falling leaf is a tiny kite
with a string too small to see, held
by the part of me in charge
of making beauty
out of grief.

LIFE SENTENCE

I finally have a wrist that is sharper than the blade.

NOT ALONE

In 2005, former Canadian Minister of Defense
Paul Hellyer sat before a council and said publicly
for the first time, *UFOs are as real*

as the airplanes flying overhead, said it is known
why sightings dramatically increased after the explosion
of the first atom bomb in the New Mexico desert.

Said the universe has been watching us
break our promise to be good stewards of our earth.
Before my mother ever pointed my eyes

toward the snow falling in Orion's hair,
Paul Hellyer was flying around the world trying
to keep our weapons out of space, wanted

his grandchildren to have place they could grow
a garden, didn't want them to look at the moon
and see a man's face.

Paul Hellyer asks us to stretch our minds
wide enough to see our solar system
is only a dot inside of a dot inside of a dot.

The Milky Way is one of nine-hundred-billion
atoms in a grain of sand on the beach
of the universe. I believe Paul Hellyer

because I've seen some magic in my life—
and not all of it is from here, this curveball
of a planet we are so convinced cannot be hit.

We call the weather *beautiful*
because there are no more snowmen in Colorado,
but there are men with cold hearts

who buy stock in hurricanes and tsunamis.
Who buy stock in war and cancer
and poverty. Who buy stock

in extinction. Whenever I wake up
thinking: *No one is going to win*
the human race—we are all going

to lose unless something changes soon,
I give myself   space.

I remember the most effective remedy
      for my depression is being told I am not alone.
          And I know we are not alone

better than Pythagoras knew the earth
      wasn't flat. Knew you couldn't walk to the edge
          of it and fall off. Go far enough

and you simply run into something
      you couldn't imagine existed—
          the coral reefs, or the lavender fields

of France, or the bayous of Louisiana
      at dusk, or the lone aspen tree that's right now
          tapping on my living room window,

its autumn leaves blinking
      like two thousand yellow lights
          begging me to slow down

and know the truth is a planet
    we haven't discovered yet.
        But it has discovered us.

Someone tells me Paul Hellyer has gone off
    the deep end—but is the shallow end
        where I'm meant to stay?

What does it mean to be grounded in reality?
    How many senses have I had to shut down
        to have common sense?

I don't want my sense to be common,
    to pace a cubicle of conditioning—my dreams
        limited to a nap, my consciousness

sold to the same folks buying extinction.
    I don't know how to save the world,
        but questions themselves are telescopes.

I know there is medicine in knowing
    how much we don't know. I know
        there are answers in being awestruck.

I know someone, somewhere,
is pointing to a speck of light
that is our tiny blue planet

and saying, *I bet*
that planet is capable
of sustaining life.

And for now, they'd be right.

HOW I BECAME A POET

Fifth grade, basketball tryouts.
Me—the tiniest kid in my class,
haircut so strange I looked
like a third-grade boy who got picked on
by his first-grade brother.

Sprinting from the sideline
to center court, I fell down
two times—because planes can't fly
with the pilot's eyes on the wings,
and I couldn't run

without staring at my shoes,
my brand-new shoes, white
as Isiah Thomas' teeth
when he smiled, and he always
smiled, soaring toward the rim

like a kite, the other team's coach
screaming for a second string.
If I'd been Jordan, I might have called
my shoes *fly* like Jordan flew,
the whole world staring at his wings,

the whole world falling at his feet,
but I was who I was, so I said, Neat.
These shoes are so neat, I said
to my mom, begging her
to buy them the night before tryouts

in Ames department store,
which was just as good
as the stores they had in towns
big enough to have malls.
But I was from Calais, Maine,

spelled like Calais, France,
said like the rough patches
on all the millworkers' hands.
You could fit the whole town of Calais
into Madison Square Garden

seven times, meaning I could have
seven seats all my own to watch
Patrick Ewing's hook shot
turn the defense into the kind of fish
my uncles would catch and throw back

because they were just too small.
Calais was known for being the first town
to receive the distress signal
that the Titanic was going down
and not getting there in time,

so I arrived to the gym early
and watched my new shoes float
from the locker room to the bleachers
where I counted seventy-four seats—
sixty-four if everyone were the size

of Larry Bird or Hakeem Olajuwon
or Muggsy Bogues's heart, or Charles Barkley
who I loved watching because he always threw
tantrums like a kid, and I liked knowing
I could still be myself

when I grew up.
I was on the baseline waiting
for the coach to blow the whistle
for the sprint when Jamie Lorde threw
a chest pass of words directly at my face:

Andrea's wearing plastic shoes!
she belted, until I was triple teamed
by laughter, the other kids repeating,
Andrea's got plastic shoes!
Up until then I hadn't known

what leather was. Didn't know the rule
that killing something made it worth more
and my shoes had never screamed
and therefore would never bleed
the word *cool* all over the court.

For a moment, basketball was a moon
I wished I could deflate to turn back
the calendar to Ames department store
right before my mother's crescent grin
said, *Yeah, kiddo, those shoes*

are pretty neat. I guess
you can have them. But I couldn't
turn back time, so I tried to think of something
smart to say. Something Magic
Johnson would have said

if trash talking had earned him his name.
But I was a mismatch for Mean, had no chance
of blocking Mean's shots. Mean jab-stepped,
and I was fooled into my benching joy,
into benching the truth

that I loved my new shoes
more than Isiah Thomas loved his teeth
when he bit the cork off the champagne
three years in a row for Detroit,
a city that would keep those trophies

as their gold when the last factory
closed its doors. In the fifth grade, defense
was still the weakest part of my game,
so hit by a hard foul of laughter
I ignored my heart's referee,

looked at Jaime Lorde and then down
at the floor and said, *I hate these shoes.*
I hate them. They're just the stupid ones
I'm wearing until my good ones
come in the mail.

And maybe it was something about knowing
it wouldn't be the first time I'd deny loving
something I loved, but when the coach
blew the whistle, I ran in my plastic shoes
like it was 1912

and I was gonna get to the Titanic
in time, like I was gonna make my town
famous for sinking nothing
but baskets at the buzzer.
I ran like everyone but me

had something dead on their feet
and kept running that fast
for the next eight years, all the way
to the state championship
in a city so big

it had a mall, and I cut down
the net with my smile just like Isiah's
and carried the first gold ball
  back to the hands of a town
whose calluses for that entire night

disappeared. And the next week
in the mail, I got a letter from the college
I had dreamed of playing ball at ever since
the ball had been bigger than me,
and because I knew I wasn't allowed

to spend four years
studying only my jump shot,
I said, *I guess I'll learn*
to write some poems
while I'm here.

SEE THIS THROUGH

Opening to Andrea's live show "Right Now, I Love You Forever"

San Francisco—so many years ago the queers could still afford
to live there—I was in a woman's bed, wrapped up in her sheets,
when she stood naked on top of the mattress and began to peel
the glow-in-the-dark stars off the ceiling, pressing constellations
all over her skin. Cassiopeia on her collarbone. Orion on her wrist.
She said, *I could be your universe*—and I made my wish.

But it didn't come true.

My therapist, who I can never go a day without
quoting, has a theory about love. She says often we are believing
a lie when we believe time is what helps us see each other more
clearly. Says to consider the opposite might be true. Consider
the beginning might actually be when our hearts have perfect vision.

> Remember when she left her red sock
> in your white laundry and you knew
> you'd never stop blushing?

> Remember when her laughter was a disco ball
> and everything around her sparkled—
> especially you.

> Remember when you could find no flaws,
> just quirks you would have worn
> on a charm bracelet.

How you told her you were terrified
of loud noises and she snuck the balloons out
of every birthday party you went to.

You adored that she ate doughnuts
for every breakfast, called naps *snoozers*, built
her countertops from old chess boards.

You watched her fold your horoscope
into a paper airplane you hoped
had no exit row.

Found sixty-four lucky pennies
in the five months after you met,
wrapped them for her birthday in fabric
you cut from the sleeve of your only warm jacket,

learned to play the ukulele
just so you write her songs,

tattooed her halos on your arms
and left a space for all
you'd both do wrong.

You sneeze poetry, you said to her.
*You could win the Nobel Prize
just from getting the flu.*

What if what you saw then was the truth? My therapist asks.
Your holiest self seeing someone else's holiest self? What if
what came after was the lie? What if the disco ball never stopped
sparkling, something just closed your eyes? Your past, maybe?
The terror you carry inside? The *not enough* or *too much*
that raised you to do everything you could to ensure
you'd be hurt more than you'd be loved.

* * *

We were in our kitchen in New Orleans.
It was morning and I was sitting at the table
her grandfather had given her grandmother
as a wedding gift when she told me where her lips

had been the night before. I walked into our bedroom,
picked up the sixty-four pennies and threw them
out the door. She dove to the ground, crawled

on her knees, counting the pennies one by one
into her hands, saying my name over and over,
both of our lips buried in tears.

When we officially broke up, I was so certain I had nothing
left to lose I went to an open mic for the first time and read
a love poem I wrote for her before we said goodbye.

I was shaking so much my voice could not be heard
over the paper rattling in my hands, but I knew
wherever she was in the world that night
the poem found her ears.

That was twenty years ago.
Twenty years I've been writing love poems.

Last night I was at her house holding her son who calls me *Ankle*
because it's a mix between *aunt* and *uncle*, and I was thinking
how the straight folks in my life don't always understand
why so many of my exes are my closest friends

but how my therapist says it's the most beautiful
part of the queer community—how we've all lost so much family
when we find people we call family, we'll do almost
anything to not say goodbye.

And because I didn't say goodbye, she was there
when I met the woman dressed in glow-in-the-dark stars,
and the woman with the checkerboard countertops,
and the woman who rescued me from balloons,

and the woman whose halos I tattooed,
and the woman who ate ice cream with her hands
and I didn't call it a flaw. I called it a quirk,
and my god—I know that makes it sound like I got around.

(Let me say for the record I wish I got around.)
But I didn't. I'm just old and I wrote it all down.
Every bit of it: the love who came out to her family
in the middle of Thanksgiving grace.

The woman whose eyes were the mirror
where I learned to love my own face.
The day I got proposed to hours after
leaving the psych ward, the stitches still raw

in my arm, how unready I was to let myself be loved
by someone who thought, even at my lowest,
I shined the sun—my therapist[1] is still working
with me on that one.

---

1   My therapist's name is Julie. I had a crush on a woman named Julie once.
I sent her a text that said, You have the same name as my therapist—I'm
wondering if I could come lie down on your couch sometime. I was so proud
of that text. I would have been prouder had I not accidentally sent it to Julie
the therapist instead.

THE LAST HOURS

We've been dating only two weeks when the phone rings in the middle of the night. I beg every light green on my way to her house, and the grief gods answer. When I reach her, she is curled up in the garden. The earth is under her nails as if she's just discovered something that could have fed the whole world wasn't harvested in time. She says nothing for almost half an hour then whispers, *My grandpa died.* The moon flickers out like a candle.

* * *

Our second date was a walk through a neighborhood where the porches were bigger than both of our homes combined. *Does it thrill you or crush you to know no one inside is more grateful than us*—I would have asked if I hadn't known the answer. If the answer wasn't the reason I loved her already.

Because that night was the first time my eyes weren't too shy to look directly at her face, I finally noticed the gap in her teeth on Mapleton street, beside a house shaped like a wedding cake. *My grandparents have been married for sixty-three years,* she told me, and a door in the center of her smile opened to a tiny Midwest church in 1944. At the end of the aisle—two kids, too young to know anything, were promising each other everything.

* * *

Now tonight, this simple garden is its own church as she tells me about the last hours of her grandfather's life. *He was in bed,* she says. *My grandma was sitting beside him, holding his hand. He said the word,* love. *Then a few minutes later he said it again. And then he kept saying it:* Love love love, *over and over for hours. He said it for hours then kissed my grandma goodbye.* There are enough tears between us to pull a redwood tree out of a nettle seed or to water the garden beneath us for a century.

Six years from now, we will kiss for the last time. Seven years from now, we will take our first walk together as friends. Eight years from now, a bicycle accident will shatter her two front teeth and I'll beg her not to let the dentist fill the gap. She won't listen, but the door to the church will stay open anyway. Each time she smiles, a bouquet of wildflowers will fly from her grandmother's twenty-two-year-old hand and move through the air in slow motion, trying to find a way to land in the arms of the whole world.

* * *

I've written so many poems in my life. And every single one of them was just trying to find a better way to say what one soul said to another soul with one word. Isn't it amazing that I came up so short? Isn't it everything that I tried so hard and failed to write a single thing more beautiful than

love.

button
poetry

Acknowledgements

Thank you, Meg, for your love, humor, and willingness to keep editing my writing in spite of my teary tantrums. Thank you, Mandy, for your soft, tough, and eternal heart. Thank you, Emily, Bethy, Denise, Buddy, Eve, Natalie, Lauren, Manny, Siaara, Chris, Laura, Alia, Sandi, Sonya, Shannon, Julia. Thank you, Mom & Dad. Thank you, Mika and Greg for helping me bring "Homesick" into the world. Thank you, Liza, for your activism, grace, and the heart-lessons that will never ever leave me. Thank you, Lara. Thank you, Daniel and Carolyn Kinderlehrer. Thank you, Julie. Thank you to the incredible Button team: Tanesha, Sam, Riley. Thank you, Safia Elhillo, for your wise and thoughtful editing. Thank you, Amy Law, for your design genius. Thank you, Alyssa. Thank you, Susie. Thank you, Heather, for far too much to list here, so thank you for everything. Thank you, Marilyn and the Mercury Cafe. Thank you, Derrick and Write Bloody Publishing, for believing in me long before I believed in myself.

"To Whom It Definitely Concerns" and "Acceptance Speech After Setting the World Record in Goosebumps" were written based on prompts from Megan Falley's writing workshop *Poems That Don't Suck*.

"Instead of Depression" was inspired by a conversation with my therapist Julie, as was just about every other poem in the book.

"The Museum of Broken Relationships" was inspired by my ex and now dear friend, journalist Shannon Service, and her article "Hurts So Good: Considering Love and Science at the Museum of Broken Relationships," which I really recommend reading. Additionally, please check out the Museum of Broken Relationships at Brokenships.com.

"See This Through" includes lines previously published in *Lord of the Butterflies* (Button Poetry, 2018) and *Pansy* (Write Bloody Publishing, 2015).

"The Year of No Grudges" includes lines previously published in *Take Me With You* (Penguin/Plume, 2018).

About the Author

Andrea Gibson (they/them/theirs) is a queer author of five full-length collections of poetry. Their book *Lord of the Butterflies* (Button Poetry, 2018) was the winner of The Independent Publisher's Award as well as a Good Reads Choice Award Finalist. In 2018, Penguin Books published *Take Me With You*, an illustrated collection of Gibson's most beloved quotes, and in 2019, Gibson co-authored their first nonfiction endeavor *How Poetry Can Change Your Heart* (Chronicle Books). Andrea served as the editor of *We Will Be Shelter* (Write Bloody Publishing, 2014), an anthology of social justice poetry whose proceeds are donated annually to nonprofits working to dismantle systems of oppression. Best known for their live performances, they have spent much of the last fifteen years on tour, often filling large-capacity rock clubs, thus helping to revolutionize the way poetry is appreciated culturally. In addition to their written work, Gibson has released seven full-length spoken word albums in collaboration with celebrated musicians. Their work strives to be a lifeline to the lonely, a megaphone in spaces of dangerous silence, and a permission slip to feel it all.

OTHER BOOKS BY BUTTON POETRY

If you enjoyed this book, please consider checking out some of our others, below. Readers like you allow us to keep broadcasting and publishing. Thank you!

Neil Hilborn, *Our Numbered Days*
Hanif Abdurraqib, *The Crown Ain't Worth Much*
Sabrina Benaim, *Depression & Other Magic Tricks*
Rudy Francisco, *Helium*
Rachel Wiley, *Nothing Is Okay*
Neil Hilborn, *The Future*
Phil Kaye, *Date & Time*
Andrea Gibson, *Lord of the Butterflies*
Blythe Baird, *If My Body Could Speak*
Desireé Dallagiacomo, *SINK*
Dave Harris, *Patricide*
Michael Lee, *The Only Worlds We Know*
Raych Jackson, *Even the Saints Audition*
Brenna Twohy, *Swallowtail*
Porsha Olayiwola, *i shimmer sometimes, too*
Jared Singer, *Forgive Yourself These Tiny Acts of Self-Destruction*
Adam Falkner, *The Willies*
George Abraham, *Birthright*
Omar Holmon, *We Were All Someone Else Yesterday*
Rachel Wiley, *Fat Girl Finishing School*
Bianca Phipps, *crown noble*
Rudy Francisco, *I'll Fly Away*
Natasha T. Miller, *Butcher*
Kevin Kantor, *Please Come Off-Book*
Ollie Schminkey, *Dead Dad Jokes*
Reagan Myers, *Afterwards*
L.E. Bowman, *What I Learned From the Trees*
Patrick Roche, *A Socially Acceptable Breakdown*

Available at buttonpoetry.com/shop and more!

OTHER BOOKS BY ANDREA GIBSON

Take Me With You
How Poetry Can Change Your Heart
Lord of the Butterflies
The Madness Vase
Pansy
Pole Dancing to Gospel Hymns

FORTHCOMING BOOKS BY BUTTON POETRY

Rachel Wiley, *Revenge Body*
Ebony Stewart, *BloodFresh*
Ebony Stewart, *Home.Girl.Hood.*
Kyle 'Guante' Tran Myhre, *Not a lot of Reasons to Sing, but Enough*
Steven Willis, *A Peculiar People*
Topaz Winters, *So, Stranger*
Siaara Freeman, *Urbanshee*
Junious 'Jay' Ward, *Composition*
Darius Simpson, *Never Catch Me*
Robert Lynn, *How to Maintain Eye Contact*